TAE KWON DO

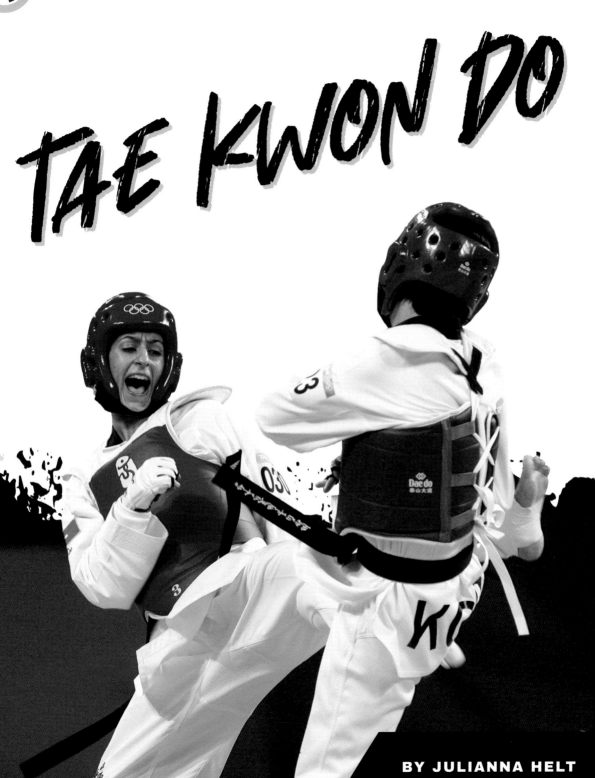

BY JULIANNA HELT

Apex is distributed by North Star Editions:
sales@northstareditions.com | 888-417-0195

Produced for Apex by Red Line Editorial.

Photographs ©: Themba Hadebe/AP Images, cover; Shutterstock Images, 1, 4–5, 6, 8, 9, 14, 15, 16–17, 18–19, 20, 21, 22–23, 24, 25, 26–27, 29; Kyodo News/AP Images, 10–11; PJF Military Collection/Alamy, 13

Library of Congress Control Number: 2023910147

ISBN
978-1-63738-768-9 (hardcover)
978-1-63738-811-2 (paperback)
978-1-63738-893-8 (ebook pdf)
978-1-63738-854-9 (hosted ebook)

Printed in the United States of America
Mankato, MN
012024

NOTE TO PARENTS AND EDUCATORS
Apex books are designed to build literacy skills in striving readers. Exciting, high-interest content attracts and holds readers' attention. The text is carefully leveled to allow students to achieve success quickly. Additional features, such as bolded glossary words for difficult terms, help build comprehension.

TABLE OF CONTENTS

CHAPTER 1

TESTING DAY

A student arrives at tae kwon do class. Today is testing day. The student is trying to earn a new belt.

Schools where students take tae kwon do classes are called dojangs.

First, the student shows the moves she has learned. The moves create a series called a form. The student does each move carefully. A group of judges watch her.

FAST FACT

One form may include dozens of moves.

When doing forms, students must do each move in the right order.

When testing for some belts, students only do forms. For more-advanced belts, students also need to spar.

Next, the student **spars**. The judges watch her fight with her partner. The student's strikes and blocks **impress** them. They give her a new color of belt.

THE DOBOK

Tae kwon do uses a uniform called a dobok. A belt ties around it. The belt's color shows the person's skill level. Students start with white belts. They get new colors as they gain skills.

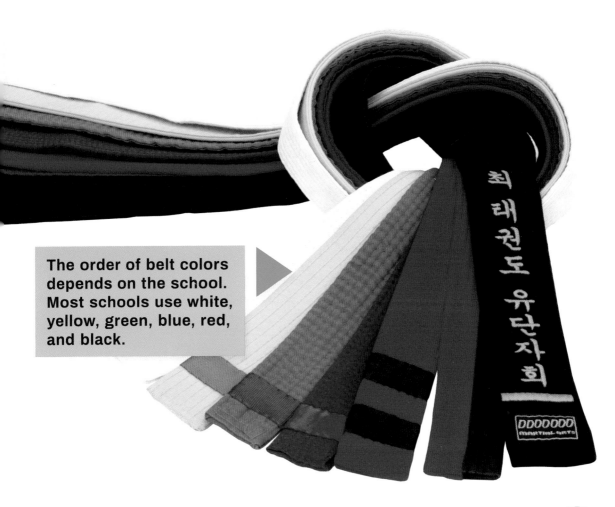

The order of belt colors depends on the school. Most schools use white, yellow, green, blue, red, and black.

CHAPTER 2

History

Tae kwon do comes from Korea. It is at least 2,000 years old. People first created it for **self-defense**. It was later used to train soldiers, too.

People in Korea's Koguryo Kingdom built tombs. One tomb has paintings of people doing tae kwon do.

Over time, many different styles developed. In 1955, a group of teachers gathered. They agreed to combine styles. They formed one **modern** version.

STRONG SKILLS

Teachers often held **demonstrations**. They showed off their skills. In 1952, South Korea's president watched one. He was impressed. He had Korean soldiers start learning tae kwon do.

Korean soldiers demonstrate their tae kwon do skills in 1979.

The best fighters travel to events around the world.

The new style spread quickly. People around the world watched and studied it. In the 1960s and 1970s, many international events began.

Every four years, top fighters compete in the Olympics.

CHAPTER 3

FiSTS AND FEET

Tae kwon do uses many types of kicks. Many involve spins or jumps. People's feet often go high into the air.

Tae kwon do is known for its high kicks.

Students also study strikes and punches. They practice hitting with lots of power. And they learn to block and **dodge**.

BLACK BELTS

Many tae kwon do schools use 18 to 20 levels. The top 9 or 10 levels are black belts. Earning these belts can take years of practice. For each one, people must learn more than 80 moves.

The forms people learn are called *poomsae* in Korean.

To stay safe when sparring, people often wear guards on their heads, legs, and chests.

Students often spar with partners. They practice ways to attack and defend. Each fighter tries to strike their partner's head and **torso**.

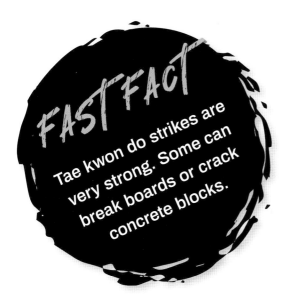

When training, people may kick pads or targets. This helps partners stay safe.

CHAPTER 4

TAE KWON DO TODAY

Today, more than 30 million people practice tae kwon do. Some use it for self-defense. Many **compete**.

Some people travel to compete in events around the world. Others go to watch.

People earn points based on the type of kick or punch and the part of the body it hits.

At sparring events, pairs of people fight matches. Each match is split into three rounds. Fighters earn points for kicks or punches.

OTHER EVENTS

Not all events involve sparring. At form competitions, people do sets of moves. Judges watch and give points. At other events, people use kicks and strikes to break boards.

At board-breaking events, people often do difficult jumps and spins. They can earn points for strength and speed.

At the world championships, the best fighters earn medals.

The fighter with the most points at the end wins. Top fighters go on to big events, such as the world **championships**.

FAST FACT

If fighters tie, a fourth round is added. The first fighter who scores wins.

COMPREHENSION QUESTIONS

Write your answers on a separate piece of paper.

1. Write a few sentences describing the main ideas of Chapter 3.

2. If you competed in tae kwon do, which type of event would you choose? Why?

3. What is a form?

    A. a set of moves done in a row

    B. a fight between two students

    C. a move that breaks a board

4. Why might black belts take years to earn?

    A. They are some of the first belts.

    B. Many other belts come first.

    C. Few other belts require learning patterns of moves.

5. What does **combine** mean in this book?

*They agreed to **combine** styles. They formed one modern version.*

    A. split apart
    B. blend together
    C. add more schools

6. What does **international** mean in this book?

*People around the world watched and studied it. In the 1960s and 1970s, many **international** events began.*

    A. no longer happening
    B. involving just one country
    C. involving many countries

Answer key on page 32.

GLOSSARY

championships
The top competitions in a league or sport.

compete
To try to beat others in a game or event.

demonstrations
Events where people show off their skills.

dodge
To move out of the way.

impress
To please or surprise someone by doing something very well.

modern
Made or used today.

self-defense
Ways to fight back or stay safe if attacked.

spars
Fights with another person as a sport or for practice.

torso
The middle part of the body that includes the chest, belly, and back.

TO LEARN MORE

BOOKS

Corso, Phil. *Tae Kwon Do*. New York: PowerKids Press, 2020.

Krohn, Frazer Andrew. *MMA: Heroic History*. Minneapolis: Abdo Publishing, 2023.

Osborne, M. K. *Combat Sports.* Mankato, MN: Amicus, 2020.

ONLINE RESOURCES

Visit **www.apexeditions.com** to find links and resources related to this title.

ABOUT THE AUTHOR

Julianna Helt is a former children's librarian turned children's book author. She enjoys researching and writing about all sorts of topics. She lives in Pittsburgh with her husband, two teenagers, and three cats.

INDEX

ANSWER KEY:
1. Answers will vary; 2. Answers will vary; 3. A; 4. B; 5. B; 6. C